President Trump and Our Post-Secular Future

How the 2016 Election Signals
the Dawning of a
Conservative Nationalist Age

Stephen R. Turley, Ph.D.

TURLEY TALKS

A New Conservative Age is Rising
www.TurleyTalks.com

Table of Contents

Introduction: The Dawning of a New Era   7

Part I: Globalism and the Nationalist Blowback

Chapter 1 The Conditioners: C.S. Lewis' Vision of "The Establishment"   15

Chapter 2 The Fall of Globalism? The Worldwide Nationalist Blowback   23

Chapter 3 "Call Me 'Mr. Brexit'": The Candidacy of Donald Trump   29

Part II President Trump and Our Post-Secular Future

Chapter 4 President Trump and the Global Religious Right   39

Chapter 5 President Trump and America's Post-Secular Future   45

Chapter 6 Trump, Education, and the Coming "War on Science"   49

Chapter 7 Nationalism and the Coming Pro-Life Spring   53

Chapter 8 Feminist Futility: Why the Women's March Promises a More Conservative Future   57

Conclusion   61

About www.TurleyTalks.com   67

About the Author   69

The Dawning of a New Era

Let's begin with a question: What is the significance of one of the most politically incorrect men on the planet being elected president of the U.S.? No matter how we answer that question, I think we have to conclude at least in part that for a vast number of Americans, political correctness simply no longer carries the same weight it used to. Think about it: We've heard over and over again that a Republican simply couldn't be elected president without adopting some form of immigration reform and amnesty, that is, without some recourse to political correctness; yet, here we had a GOP candidate spouting what many considered the most anti-immigration rhetoric we've heard in recent years, one that included at one point an all-out ban on Muslims .... *and he won*!

This leads to another question: Why has political correctness lost its power? Why has it eroded in the way it has for so many? In the pages that follow, I want to argue that the waning of political correctness is part of a much wider phenomenon, as is the election of Donald Trump. They both point to dynamics far bigger than any one thing or person, dynamics that are forging what I am calling a *post-secular age.*

Secularism and the Post-Secular

In understanding Trump's presidency as part of an emerging post-secular society, I think it helpful if we first understand secularization and why Trump's presidency indicates its increasing rejection.

Secularization is generally defined as the process by which religious ideas, institutions, and interpretations lose their social significance. Thus, at it's most basic level, the *post-*secular refers simply to the return of religion and religious values in the public square, which we are indeed witnessing throughout the world: Shintoism in Japan, Orthodoxy in Russia, Hinduism in India, Confucianism in China, and the like. And yet, scholars are often at a loss as to *why* religion is currently making a comeback; what's behind the renewal of religion, and why are post-secular dynamics so operative today?

My answer to this question involves situating the return of religion within more complex social dynamics. I argue that the return of religion is itself part of a larger worldwide nationalist, populist, and traditionalist blowback against the anticultural processes of globalization and its secular aristocracy. These nationalist, populist, and traditionalist trends are undermining the fundamental tenets of secularization and in effect forging the emergence of a post-secular world.

Scholars have long recognized that secularization is rooted in the notion of modernity. Modernity is comprised of the philosophical commitment to scientific rationalism as the sole objective mechanism for political, economic, and cultural management. Rooted in such rationalism, modernity sees all pre-modern societies, particularly those governed by religious commitments, as inherently irrational, and thus asserts itself as the one true political, economic, and cultural meaning system for all nations and peoples. In the twentieth-century, the West has proclaimed liberal democracy as the ultimate political system, the Soviet East proclaimed communism as the ultimate economic system, and Italy and Germany declared fascism as the ultimate cultural meaning system.

With the death of fascism and communism, the liberal democratic West declared itself to be the true global champion of all three systems: political, economic, and cultural. The chief export of this Western triumphalism has been what is commonly referred to as *globalization.* Globalization involves the interaction between capitalism, urbanization, technology, and telecommunications within a mass transnational economic system. For example, we all know today that what happens with the Nikkei on the Tokyo stock exchange has ripple effects on the European markets which in turn affect Wall Street which comes back to Tokyo. This is the mass global economy known as globalization.

However, there is a significant cost that comes with this standardized political, economic, and cultural system: Globalization entails processes that negate borders, localized economies, and traditions. It negates borders with its transnational flow of goods and international standardized regulations; it negates local industry with a global division of labor that relocates manufacturing to the global south; and it negates traditions through what is called disembedding, which dislodges culture away from localized control. This disembedding has replaced traditional moral norms with highly secular, consumer-based lifestyle values, at the center of which is the autonomous individual who exercises sovereign control over his or her own life circumstances. Such secularized sovereignty includes the right to determine one's own religion, culture, and even gender.

It is no wonder, then, that in response to globalism and its aggressive secularization, we're seeing a mass worldwide blowback. As it turns out, not everyone wants this one-size-fits-all standardized economy and consumerist culture. And this is because, like in the Soviet East or Fascist Germany, modernity in the West has largely died. Less and less Westerners believe in the absolutist vision of scientific rationalism and personal autonomy. Few today believe in a one-size-fits-all political, economic, and cultural system.

And so, the roots of modernity have died even although the West continues to export globalization to the rest of the world. This means that, in one sense, secular globalization is more powerful than ever before, in that its global reach is farther and wider than ever, and yet it is also weaker than it's ever been, in that its modernist roots have all but rotted out. And because the roots have died, more and more populations are looking inward, turning to nation, culture, and tradition as the basis for a post-modern, post-globalist, and, indeed, a post-secular social order.

Thus, we find ourselves in the midst of a mass worldwide dialectic, in that while at one level society is indeed becoming more secular, in that globalization remains the West's chief export, at another level there is a traditionalist and nationalist blowback to that globalized secularity. A post-secular analysis of the world recognizes this dialectic and observes the extent to which secular norms and tenets are increasingly rejected and resisted. Examples of such religious resurgence abound: In political activism, the so-called Christian Right are more energized, organized, and engaged than ever before; in education, we are seeing public monies funding Christian as well as Buddhist curriculum; in the media we are seeing the illusion of objective reporting crumble, such that news is now widely held to be a central place of political contestation; our immigration policy is excluding certain Muslim populations in the name of national security; pro-abortion sensibilities are being increasingly replaced with pro-life sentiments and legislation; and the threat of terrorism is turning citizens of the U.S. more and more toward nationalist-right politics.

For many people in this country, on both the political left and right, secularized political correctness simply doesn't cut it anymore; secular social arrangements don't offer the solutions necessary for dealing with the variant adversities of our age. And with this impoverishment, people are turning towards either a civic nationalism, as is the case with Trump and his supporters, or more to a micro-ethnic nationalism, as is the case with the Black Lives Matter movement. In both cases, the inclusive tolerance that supposedly marks a secularized multicultural vision of life is withering away and, with it, we are seeing the erosion of a major tenet of secularization.

With the present shift towards nationalism, it should be noted that the post-secular does not necessarily mean a return of Christian society and values. The church does need to be very wary of the temptations of becoming a mere surrogate for a neo-nationalist movement. The jury is still out as to whether the church is going to be exploited by this resurgent nationalism or whether the church now has a voice that it did not have in a more secularized society, to morally guide and direct this nationalism in distinctively Christian terms.

For the reasons I lay out in this book, I do believe that the election of Donald J. Trump indicates the dawning of a new era of national re-arrangements, re-definitions, and re-interpretations of many levels of society, one in which the secular assumptions of the past are being challenged and indeed usurped in ways not yet experienced. This book is an exploration of just such a post-secular horizon. It is arranged in two parts: Part I explores the worldwide clash between globalization and nationalism and how the Trump candidacy and presidency fit into such a dialectic. Part II explores a representative sampling of the various aspects constitutive of an emerging post-secular society. It is my hope that by exploring the features of a nationalist populist turn, we will recognize and better understand the fascinating time in which we find ourselves, at the dawn of a new era in our nation's history.

Part I

Globalism and the Nationalist Blowback

CHAPTER 1

The Conditioners: C.S. Lewis' Vision of "The Establishment"

The election of 2016 turned its snarl to the so-called "establishment." Whether in the guise of Donald Trump or Bernie Sanders, the campaigns with the largest and most enthusiastic crowds garnered their support by taking on the establishment.

But who or what is the establishment?

The Conditioners

Here I turn to an astonishing work, a very small book, under a hundred pages, written by the Oxford scholar C.S. Lewis, called the *Abolition of Man.* And there Lewis draws out the logic of the premises of a secularized society, which he sees as one dedicated to defining social and cultural progress in thoroughly scientific and technological terms. What Lewis noticed was that such a society would be comprised of two main classes of people, what he called the 'conditioner' class and the 'conditioned' class. What he meant by that is because the modern secular age operates according to complex technological and scientific processes, it requires a class of experts and engineers who have the specialized competency and expertise to govern this technocracy. And so, within such a modern matrix, the wider population is conditioned to believe that their health and happiness is dependent upon this ruling class of experts and engineers.

But Lewis also recognized that secular technology-based societies inevitably reject traditional moral conceptions of life. This is because technology is organized and governed by modern scientific processes which are considered value neutral and thus devoid of moral frames of reference. And so, without these moral frames of reference, the only way there can be a moral consensus in society is through some kind of manipulation. If a sense of divine obligation and hence a collective self-government has been erased, then only coercion, compulsion, and extortion can provide a motivation for ethical conformity. Thus, manipulation is at the heart of this brave new world to which we are embarking. And if manipulation is an intrinsic characteristic of modern life, then there must surface by definition two classes of people: manipulators and manipulatees, or, in Lewis' terms, the 'conditioners' and the 'conditioned'. The commitment to technological progress on the one hand and the need for coercion and manipulation in order to bring about moral conformity in an amoral world on the other, thus give rise to the formation of a social elite, a secular aristocracy, with the vast majority of the human population repositioned as objects of manipulation.

And the reason why the mass population goes along with this class division of conditioner and conditioned is because the masses have been conditioned to believe that it is this class of elite experts who maintain the social conditions necessary for

our health and happiness. So this class division is just a small toll that we pay for all of these wonderful benefits of living in a modern society.

Globalization and Disembedding Our Traditions

Now, in many respects, Lewis' predictive theory has been realized in the mass conglomerate of processes known by scholars as *globalization.* As we noted above, globalization involves the interaction between capitalism, urbanization, technology, and telecommunications within a mass transnational economic system. What's important here is that globalization involves something called *disembedding,* which in effect propels economic activity away from localized control toward far more transnational control. So here I like to use the example of your local shopping mall: In one sense, the mass shopping complex is in fact local in terms of its proximity to consumers; but notice that the retail outlets that comprise the various stores at a mall are *not* local but rather national and international chains and brands. Notice, too, the movies that are playing at the mall's theater; these are hardly the product of local acting talent.

But scholars have noticed that this disembedding is not limited to the economic; such dislodging also involves localized customs, traditions, languages, and religions. For example, when we see so-called 'mom and pop stores' closing and malls and franchise chains opening, traditional ways of life, customary moral codes and relationships are closing up as well. And what that means is that traditional moral conceptions are becoming increasingly difficult to sustain in the midst of a globalized world.

So, whereas traditional societies are characterized generally by very sacred beliefs and practices that have been handed down from generation to generation, globalized societies come in and offer a mass range of consumer-based options that call into question the sanctity of those traditional beliefs and practices, relativizing them to a 'global food court' of many other creedal alternatives.

I'm sure you've seen the holiday comedy classic, *A Christmas Story.* There's a scene when, after the Christmas Turkey was eaten by some local dogs, the Parker family goes to a local Chinese restaurant for Christmas dinner. As the waiters attempt (unsuccessfully) to sing "Deck the Halls" to create a more festive atmosphere, a roast duck is carried over to the family's table, with its head still attached. "It's a beautiful duck," the father says to the waiter incredulously, "but it's smiling at me!" After the waiter abruptly decapitates the duck with a meat cleaver, the narrator remarks: "That Christmas would live in our memories as the Christmas when we were introduced to Chinese Turkey. All was right with the world."

What this scene points out is that in globalized societies, our local customs and traditions can be exchanged for wider translocal options and practices. The Christmas Turkey can be replaced by Peking Duck, and it doesn't matter; it's ok if we haven't done this before. What makes tradition so special anyway?

The Age of Lifestyle Values

Now what all of this means is that globalization radically changes our conception of what it means to be human. Globalist societies tend to think of the human person as a consumer. Again, traditional social structures and arrangements are generally fixed in terms of key identity markers such as gender, sexual orientation, and religious affiliation. But globalized societies, because of the wide array of options, see this fixedness as restrictive. And so traditional morals and customs tend to give way to what we called *lifestyle values*. Lifestyle values operate according to a plurality of what sociologist Peter Berger defines as 'life-worlds,' wherein each individual practices whatever belief system deemed most plausible by him or her. These belief systems include everything from religious identity to gender identity.

We are living in a time when a moral conception of life has been replaced with a consumerist conception of life; traditional values and beliefs have been eclipsed by lifestyle values and beliefs. And the key here is that these lifestyle values and beliefs were created and are sustained by a consumerist globalized economy. So, we can see why CEOs tend to have a vested interest in promoting alternative lifestyles, like what we've seen with the boycotts against North Carolina's bathroom law that requires men to use the men's room; alternative lifestyles buy more and more products that help the person reinvent him or herself in accordance with the chosen lifestyle.

Legal Convenience

And at the level of politics, globalized societies tend to redefine the whole notion of the rule of law, especially in C.S. Lewis' terms of the conditioners and the conditioned. While traditional societies viewed human law as something reflective of transcendent divine law, modern societies actually invent law, they make it up in accordance with the needs of social conditions as the elite class of conditioners understands and interprets them.

And so, in modern societies, there are two fundamentally different relationships to the law. While the conditioned, in C.S. Lewis' terms, are always *under* the law, in that we don't invent but are called only to comply, the conditioners are always *above* the law, since they invent law in such a way that complies with their own social management and engineering.

You see, in a society where laws are made up by a class of elites, it's not a coincidence that those elites tend to benefit from those laws and their variant interpretations.

But wait a minute: why aren't people up in arms about this? Arbitrary laws? Where are the mass protests over the injustice of such a thing?

Ah, don't forget: we're the conditioned class. We've been conditioned to believe that it is experts like the so-called establishment who maintain the social conditions necessary for our health and happiness. This is just a small toll that we pay for all of these wonderful benefits of living in a modern society.

Lewis' predictive theory is very much in accord with the detraditionalizing processes of globalization which have in effect reconstituted life around a secular aristocracy, a class of technological, business, and political 'experts' that are considered indispensable to our highest happiness and freedom. And Lewis recognized that this is precisely the genius of the modern age: that our freedoms are absolutely dependent on keeping an elite class of conditioners in power. This is Lewis' vision of the 'establishment.'

But not everyone is happy with this arrangement. There are signs that the masses are beginning to rebel.

CHAPTER 2

The Fall of Globalism? The Worldwide Nationalist Blowback

In our last chapter, we explored the radically dehumanizing nature of globalization and the rise of what C.S. Lewis called the *conditioner class.* Through a process known as *disembedding,* globalization hollows out and erodes a culture's traditions, customs, and religions, all the while conditioning the population to rely on the expertise of a class of technocrats for their highest happiness. In this chapter, we will explore a worldwide reaction to such globalizing processes in the form of nationalism and what is called re-traditionalization.

The Brexit Blowback

On the morning of June 24, 2016, the world awoke to a changed Europe. With the so-called 'Brexit' referendum, the UK voted to leave the European Union, and as such, the EU lost one of its most important member nations. Almost immediately, there were calls from France, Italy, and the

Netherlands to hold similar referenda, jeopardizing the entire EU experiment.

There are a number of scholars who interpret the Brexit as part of a wider trend among the various nations of the world, and that trend is a turn towards nationalism and the political right. And while there are various reasons for this, it seems to be mainly fueled by a backlash against globalism and the erosion of cultural and national identity.

What we are finding is that in the face of threats to localized identity markers, people assert their national symbols and sovereignty as mechanisms of resistance against globalizing dynamics. We see that at even local levels in our backyard as it were: it seems everywhere a mall is put up, a farmers' market is not far away; fast food chains are countered with slogans encouraging us to "buy local."

And this 'buying local' has larger nationalist and indeed separatist sentiments. From Bosnia to Chechnya, Rwanda and Barundi, from South Sudan to Scotland and most recently Catalonia, populations have been turning increasingly inward for civic and cultural identity.

Nationalism and Re-traditionalization

Within these balkanizing tendencies is a process called *re-traditionalization.* Because globalization challenges the traditions and customs, the religions and languages of local cultures, its processes tend to be resisted with a counter-cultural blowback. In view of the disembedding that we explored above, people are beginning to reassert their religiosity, kinship, and national symbols as mechanisms of resistance against globalizing dynamics.

Few nations exemplify this connection between a resurgent nationalism and a revived religious tradition than the Russian Federation. There has been a self-conscious distancing from globalism by Russia, drawing inspiration instead from the ideals of a neo-Byzantium, what U.S. Naval War College professor John R. Schindler calls a "Third Rome" ideology, which involves "a powerful admixture of Orthodoxy, ethnic mysticism, and Slavophile tendencies that has deep resonance in Russian history."[1] From this admixture, Russia has emerged, in the words of a recent article, as "Europe's most God-believing nation."[2]

But Russia is just the beginning. Notice what happened recently in Poland. In a ceremony at the Church of Divine Mercy in Krakow last November 19th, the Catholic Bishops of Poland, in the presence of President Andreiz Duda and many Catholic pilgrims, officially recognized Jesus Christ as the King of Poland and called upon Him to rule over their nation, its people and their political leaders.

Of interest as well is what's going on in the pro-life, pro-family revolutions in Hungary and Croatia. Since coming into office in 2010, the Prime Minister of Hungary Viktor Orban has led the way to ratifying Hungary's constitution to define marriage as a union between man and woman, he's been on the forefront of pro-life legislation, and has brought back religious education in Hungary's public schools. And in Croatia, a recent study found that belief in God among Croats

---

[1] John R. Schindler, "Putinism and the Anti-WEIRD Coalition," http://20committee.com/2014/04/07/putinism-and-the-anti-weird-coalition/.

[2] http://www.csmonitor.com/World/Europe/2011/0506/Russia-emerges-as-Europe-s-most-God-believing-nation.

has risen from 39 percent in 1989 to 75 percent in 1996 and 82 percent in 2004. Further, even though Croatia's population has for a number of reasons declined over the years, the amount of priests studying in seminary has actually remained unchanged.[3] And we further see the moral maturity of Croats in their overwhelming support to amend their national constitution to defined marriage as between a man and woman – nearly 65 percent of the population voted to keep so called same-sex marriage permanently out of Croatia.

In Georgia, there was a relatively recent backlash against the pro-Western, pro-EU government which sought to take Eastern Orthodox curriculum out of the public schools, which galvanized Orthodox groups such as the Orthodox Parents' Union. When the elections of 2012 came along, a far more traditionalist government was elected that reinstituted Eastern Orthodox education into the public schools, where icons and Orthodox crosses are displayed throughout the school buildings. And this has been accompanied by the Georgian Orthodox Church's campaign to revitalize the family, with significant results: Georgia has gone from having one of the lowest birthrates in Eastern Europe to now one of the highest.

So, in many respects, this resurgent nationalism within the Western world may in fact mean a return to traditional Christian conceptions of life. This is because globalization entails its own futility; as we have found with the attempt to bring liberal democracy to the Middle East, few are willing to die for the mall, but they will die for the mosque; they don't

---

[3]https://www.firstthings.com/web-exclusives/2014/01/eastern-europes-christian-reawakening.

die for emancipatory politics, feminism, and LGBT rights. But the willingness to die for land, people, custom, language, and religion is seemingly universal. Though a formidable challenger, globalization appears to have no chance of overcoming such innate fidelities.

This is the mass traditionalist nationalist blowback against globalization that we are seeing all over the world. The question before us now is to what extent has such a blowback come to American shores in the presidency of Donald J. Trump. That will be the subject of our next chapter.

CHAPTER 3

"Call Me 'Mr. Brexit'": The Candidacy of Donald Trump

In our last two chapters, we looked at what many scholars believe to be the two dominant forces operative in the world today, secular globalization on the one hand and traditionalist nationalism on the other, and we looked at how the two interrelate. Because globalization involves what are called detraditionalizing dynamics, which in effect replace traditional ways of life with modern secular lifestyle values, globalization tends to provoke a mass nationalist blowback, at the heart of which is re-traditionalization, the re-emergence of a culture's religion, language, and customs.

The question I want to raise in this chapter is: To what extent were such nationalist and traditionalist sentiments at work in the 2016 election? Were the concerns that propelled the Brexit and Russian Orthodoxy and a number of other nationalist movements comparably propelling the candidacy of Donald Trump?

I think the answer to that is an emphatic 'yes,' and I want to go over with you why I believe that the nationalist waves behind the Brexit have made their way to the shores of the U.S., and it was Donald Trump more than any other candidate that rode these waves.

These nationalist and indeed populist movements have some key characteristics that defined the Trump candidacy: immigration, trade, the moral climate, and political correctness, which I shall explore below.

Immigration

Nigel Farage, one of the leaders of the Brexit movement, has commented that while our problem in the US is with *illegal* immigration, in Britain their problem is with *legal* immigration, as mandated by the EU. Because globalized economies are by nature transnational, they generally involve porous borders, transcending the boundaries of nation states. And these porous borders which serve to expedite flows of goods within a globalized economy entail a significant increase in levels of immigration, both legal and illegal, which trends along the direction of economic activity: Turks flow into Germany, Albanians ebb into Greece, North Africans into France, Pakistanis into England, and Mexicans into the U.S.

This mass immigration poses a radical threat to the languages, religions, customs, and traditions of a nation, particularly as this mass immigration is exploited by politicians. For example, in the U.S., unfettered immigration, both legal and illegal, is dramatically changing the social complexion of the nation to one favoring liberal democratic policies and preconceptions. It's not that the immigrants are themselves inclined toward liberal social issues (most are not), but they have been largely persuaded that their political advocates belong to a center-left coalition at the state and federal levels. Thus, the stream of immigration that has flowed uninterrupted over the last few decades is providing an increasingly insurmountable political demographic responsible for the advancement of left-wing social agendas. The liberal politics of California today will be those of Texas tomorrow.

And so, what we can see in the wake of unfettered immigration is a combination of concerns: nationalist concerns focus on the erosion of traditions, language, and customs due to this radical demographic sea change, and populist concerns focus on the ways in which an aristocratic political elite exploit this unfettered immigration for their own political gain. If we were to stop the flow of unfettered immigration, then we will have cut-off a significant source of left-wing power and influence. And Trump was the candidate more than any other in recent memory that was committed to such stoppage, with the apparent managerial competency to accomplish it.

So that was the first characteristic of a Trump candidacy that exemplified these worldwide nationalist and populist trends.

Trade

The second characteristic involves trade policies, another issue that concerns nationalist movements throughout the world. There has been a general commitment among both Republicans and Democrats over the last several decades to establishing and maintaining American economic prominence in the processes constitutive of *globalization*, which we defined above as a worldwide social system comprised of a capitalist economy, telecommunications, technology, and mass urbanization. It has been argued (rightly) that such economic and technological dynamics have the power to arrest control of national economies away from totalitarian projects such as the Soviet Union and communist China while simultaneously expanding economic growth and prominence among capitalistic nations.

However, what's key here is that the interactions between these economic and technological forces have forged a global division of labor, where manufacturing and industry have moved to the global South, while finance and ownership of capital has coalesced around the West. And so, what we've seen over the last few decades is this mass exodus of industrial and manufacturing jobs from the U.S. into these so-called third world or global south nations such as Mexico and China. And the workers who have lost these manufacturing jobs have been told by our economic and political elites to basically get over it since it is argued that globalization is inevitable; stop clinging to your guns and your religion and move on with your lives.

It is precisely a nationalist populist resistance to these trade deals, to this globalized division of labor, that we are seeing emerge among nations today, particularly Russia and Japan. And this of course is where Trump's economic nationalism kicks in. You have many Americans, particularly those around the Rust Belt, who are tired of trade policies that ship manufacturing and industrial jobs overseas. They would like to see the government protect their jobs rather than outsource them in the name of some globalized vision of economic freedom.

Moral Climate

A third characteristic of this global nationalist and populist trend is a concern over the moral climate of the nation. As noted above, what is crucial for us to understand is that built into globalization processes is what we've called above *detraditionalization*, or various mechanisms by which local customs and traditions are relativized to wider economic, scientific, and technocratic forces. Once social life is caught up in a global industrialized economic system, it is propelled away from traditional, national, and local practices and beliefs. In the shadow of globalized transnational policies, traditional moral codes and customs become increasingly implausible to objectively sustain.

It therefore does appear that the Reagan-inspired or perhaps better Bush-inspired conservatism of the last two-score years entails two mutually exclusive social projects: the commitment to globalization allows for modernizing dynamics that undermine the commitment to traditional moral values. This may in fact explain why otherwise conservative politicians and pundits are so hesitant to openly attack political correctness or, in the case of Chris Christie who signed a bill banning so-called 'gay conversion therapy' for teens, even embrace it.

And so, what we are hearing, particularly from nations such as the Russian Federation, is a recognition that globalization undermines the moral foundations of a nation; in undercutting a nation's traditions, customs, moral codes, and religious frameworks, globalization is in fact a threat to the perpetuation of civilizational flourishing. And so, while Trump himself certainly seemed to fall quite a bit short of these traditional moral aspirations, many believed that his proposed economic nationalism provided a plausible paradigm by which traditional moral values could be protected and preserved.

Political Correctness

A fourth characteristic of this worldwide nationalist trend is a concern over political correctness. This of course fits in with much of the detraditionalizing dynamics inherent in globalization. As the name intimates, political correctness is a secular system of values that is calibrated around the sensibilities of a political elite, which in effect defends the secular state from all alternative visions of the public, most especially that of traditional values and norms. According to political correctness, the values that are specific to the Christian vision of life are no longer welcome in our public square. *This* is the essence, the nature, the purpose of such values as tolerance, inclusivity, multiculturalism, and moral relativism. And in the name of this tolerance, supporters of the Brexit for example were called racist, nativists, and xenophobes, while at the same time you have these elites calling Colin Kaepernick and supporters of Black Lives Matter heroes.

Increasingly more and more people, particularly traditionalists, are finding themselves on the wrong side of political correctness and multiculturalism. They simply don't understand why it is that individual acts of violent force among police elicits mass generalizations about systemic racism while Muslims and Islam are deliberately distanced from individual acts of Islamic terror. Christians don't understand why white people are by definition racist and black people aren't. And they certainly don't understand why Christian bakers and florists are being shut down because they won't celebrate LGBT values. They are sick and tired of political correctness substituting for justice and equity. *And no major political figure has declared war on political correctness like Donald Trump.*

Summary

And so, these four nationalist concerns – immigration, trade, the moral climate, and political correctness – are largely what propelled the Trump phenomenon. The more I examine the Trump candidacy, the more I am convinced that he was fully aware of the global nationalist and populist dynamics he tapped into, and that his positions were far too consistent regarding the interrelationship of these dynamics for this to be a mere coincidence on his part. Trump recognized the interrelationship between unfettered immigration, economic globalization, moral degeneration, and political correctness far better than any of the other Republican candidates for president, and I think *that* is the key reason why he was able to trounce so decisively the competition for the GOP nomination. For right or wrong, what mattered to a significant number of Americans and particularly Christians is that he stood up as one of them, and declared an end to public policies that many believe have contributed inordinately to the moral and economic degeneration of our nation. Voters were looking for a new political age of nationalism, populism, and traditionalism. It is to that age we now turn.

Part II

President Trump and Our Post-Secular Future

CHAPTER 4

President Trump and the Global Religious Right

By now we are all too familiar with the refrains resounding from the mainstream media that celebrated prematurely the inevitable landslide victory of Hillary Clinton over Donald Trump. One of my favorites was from CNN's Fareed Zakaria, who predicted confidently a few weeks prior to the election that Trump would lose the election and the Republican Party would be destroyed. Zakaria went on to morally denounce what he called 'white America' and their support of ending mass immigration and preserving America's Christian heritage.

Along with such ridicule and denunciation were comparably disparaging remarks about the so-called Religious Right throughout the mainstream media. Headlines before the election such as "How the religious right embraced Trump and lost its moral authority," "Donald Trump made the Religious Right implode in less than a week," and "The Religious Right's Devotion to Donald Trump will End the Movement as We Know It," confidently and all-too gleefully asserted the death of the defenders of traditional moral values with the demise of Trump's candidacy.

The irony of course is that the electoral results on November 8 served as the occasion for the humiliation of these prognosticators and pundits. Far from imploding, the Religious Right made up over 30 percent of the voting electorate.[4] According to the Pew Research organization, white evangelical Christians voted for Trump by an utterly overwhelming margin, 81 percent to Clinton's 16 percent. And Catholic voters, too, supported Trump over Clinton by a 23-point margin, 60 percent to 37 percent.[5]

What accounts for the media's fallacious and erroneous coverage? Among many other things, the media largely failed to recognize that Trump and the Christian Right faced a common enemy: *globalists and globalization*. Thus, while the media were fixated on the discrepancy between the traditional values of conservative Christians and Trump's moral indiscretions, they overlooked the common globalizing concerns that both traditionalists and Trump shared.

Globalization is characterized as a worldwide social and economic system comprised of a capitalist economy, telecommunications, technology, and mass urbanization. It has been argued that such economic and technological dynamics have the power to arrest control of national

---

[4]http://www.breitbart.com/2016-presidential-race/2016/11/10/ralph-reed-data-show-evangelicals-catholics-delivered-key-states-trump/.
[5]http://www.pewresearch.org/fact-tank/2016/11/09/how-the-faithful-voted-a-preliminary-2016-analysis/.

economies away from totalitarian projects such as the former Soviet Union and communist China while simultaneously expanding economic growth and prominence among capitalistic nations.

However, what is crucial to understand is that built into globalization processes is what scholars have termed *detraditionalization*, or various mechanisms by which local customs and traditions are relativized to wider economic, scientific, and technocratic forces. It is no wonder then, that, beginning in the 1990s, representatives from the Religious Right began to see their domestic struggle with the ascendance of secular lifestyle values in far more globalist terms. Already in 1999, Harold O.J. Brown of the conservative Christian think tank, the Howard Center, delivered a speech at the Second World Congress entitled "Globalization and the Family," where he explained the relationship between globalization and changing social relations:

> Globalization is the concept or ideal that tells us not that small is beautiful but that small is pitiful and out of date. The nation replaces the family, as in the U.S.A., public welfare replaces the father, and instead of individual nations ... we shall create a "world community."[6]

Allan C. Carlson, also of the Howard Center, observed: "[T]he new global civilization ... is militantly secular, ferociously anti-traditional, fundamentally hostile to autonomous families, the enemy of robust marital fertility, and a threat to

---

[6] Cited in Doris Buss and Didi Herman, *Globalizing Family Values: The Christian Right and International Politics* (Minneapolis: University of Minnesota Press, 2003), 36.

the newly conceived child everywhere ... *including* the new Christian child."[7] Religious Right activism has thus increasingly considered globalists and globalization as the primary threats to traditional values. The involvement of Christian organizations such as Focus on the Family, Family Research Council, and Concerned Women for America in various United Nations policy disputes demonstrates that the international arena has become integral to the mission of the Christian Right.

Austin Ruse, president of the Catholic Family and Human Rights Institute, summarized Christian Right international activism as focused on defending and perpetuating what he calls the "three sovereignties" that are under attack: nation, church, and family. With his emphasis on nationalism, protection of Christians, and promise of appointing pro-life judges, Trump's campaign represented a mutual defense of these three sovereignties, making his candidacy a natural attraction for proponents of traditional values.

The contempt that America's secular elite has for traditional moral values seems to have blinded them to the fact that, for tens of millions of citizens worldwide, nationhood, tradition, and religion really do matter. For over a century, secularization theory has postulated that traditional religions would slowly but surely die out, having been replaced by a scientifically-inspired worldview perpetuated by unbridled technological progress. The march of globalization around the world seemed to verify such a prognosis. And yet, all throughout the world, there has been a massive blowback against these secularizing globalist dynamics. The resurgence

---

[7] Cited in Buss and Herman, *Globalizing Family Values.* 38.

of the Russian Orthodox Church, Christian nationalism in Hungary and Poland, the rise of the nationalist political parties in Western Europe, and the astounding Brexit victory, all signify that traditionalist culture matters as much today as ever. The disdain and derision with which our secular elites, particularly represented in the mainstream media, have treated traditional moral customs and culture is turning out to be the basis of their own demise; a new media conglomerate, rooted in nation, church, and family, is rising and in many respects eclipsing that of the secular globalist establishment.

The growth of nationalist populism throughout the world indicates that in many respects, the political influence of the Religious Right is just beginning. Already we are seeing global alliances forming among conservative traditionalists to push back secularizing tendencies at home and abroad. Conservative northern Anglicans have been aligning themselves jurisdictionally with their southern counterparts in Africa and Asia to combat the secularizing of sexual norms in their church. Multi-national coalitions have been formed to block anti-traditionalist measures at the United Nations. And recently Patriarch Kirill and Pope Francis signed a historic joint statement calling for an end to the global persecution of Christians by wars in the Middle East and militant secularism in Europe. The formation of a global Religious Right coalition to combat such tendencies appears to be more and more likely as political power increasingly aligns with populist sentiments.

The obituary for the Religious Right has been written and rewritten many times; this election cycle was no exception. But scholars are aware that it is a movement that is highly adaptable to changing social dynamics both domestically and abroad. The election of Donald Trump as well as the resurgence of Christianity throughout Eurasia signals that the Religious Right, rather than lying on its deathbed, may be experiencing a new birth.

CHAPTER 5

President Trump and America's Post-Secular Future

"Imagine what our country could accomplish if we started working together as one people, under one God, saluting one American flag." Donald J. Trump

In August of this year, Nate Silver, the wonder kid pollster who predicted the 2012 election with uncanny accuracy, argued that Donald Trump had only a 13 percent chance of winning the election. The prospects for such a remote victory were echoed throughout the establishment media. By November 1st, Moody Analytics predicted that Hillary would win with 332 electoral votes, which itself sparked a number of articles celebrating Clinton's inevitable coronation at the polls.

But how could the polls have been so misleading, and how could the mainstream media have been so wrong? We need to understand that the old establishment media outlets self-consciously perpetuate a secular vision of life which sees the world in terms of two groups of people: those who support a secular liberal vision of life and who are thereby rational and liberal, and those who resist a secular vision of life and who are therefore by definition irrational and repressive. So, the various establishment media and journalistic outlets are largely incapable of understanding and interacting with non-secular conceptions of life.

It is the waning of this secular vision of life that is perhaps the most significant indicator of Trump's win. We are now entering into what scholars call a *post-secular age*. As the name implies, a post-secular society is one that no longer subscribes to the two fundamental commitments of secular liberalism: scientific rationalism and personal autonomy or lifestyle values. At a very basic level, post-secular society is about the return of religion and religious values in the public square. We've seen this with the advent of Sharia councils in the U.K. that arbitrate between conflicts among Muslims, the resurgence of the Russian Orthodox Church as a major political, moral, and cultural force in the Russian Federation, the revival of imperial Shintoism at the highest levels of the Japanese government, a revitalization of Confucian philosophy among Chinese officials, Hindu nationalism in India, Islam in Turkey, and on and on.

Here in the U.S., similar processes are evident in the increasing collapse of multiculturalism and political correctness, which together represent the value system of secularization. Multiculturalism is the idea that America is made up of a plurality of cultural identities that consumer-defined individuals get to pick for themselves, with no single culture being dominant or superior. And political correctness is simply multiculturalism married to the state, wherein government policies favor some cultural or ethnic groups at the expense of others. Hence, Van Jones, on the night of Trump's victory, could spout on CNN that white people voting

their interests is racist and nativist bigotry while black people voting their interests is liberation and justice.

In many respects, this politically correct multicultural vision of life is on the brink of collapse. On the one hand, a hardline anti-immigration policy proposal – once considered the political death knell for a republican candidate – won overwhelmingly at the ballot box. On the other hand, multiculturalism is morphing into tribalization and balkanization on the political left. The Black Lives Matter movement, for example, is nothing less than an ethno-nationalist movement, a kind of absolutist tribalization that rejects secular notions of tolerance and inclusivity. Secular multicultural and tolerance norms are collapsing all over the place, not merely due to the wave of nationalist populist sentiments on the right, but also due to the split allegiances that occur as the result of multiculturalism.

Moreover, this turn towards nationalist sentiments that we are seeing all over the globe actually entails a resurgence of historic religious identities and moral commitments, largely due to the interrelationship between nationalism and revitalized traditions. In the face of threats to localized or national identity by globalized secular processes, populations tend to reassert symbols of cultural identity such as language, custom, tradition, and religion as mechanisms of resistance.

We can see evidence of a revitalized civic religion here at home. In his recent campaign speech in Main, Trump said: "Imagine what our country could accomplish if we started working together as one people, under one God, saluting one

American flag." This became a refrain in his campaign speeches: one people under one God. And while some can't get past the potential threat to religious freedom such a hypothetical statement represents, we have to understand that this is precisely the kind of revitalization of public religion that accompanies the ascendancy of nationalist sentiments.

Moreover, Trump is putting such a vision into policy. He is promising to repeal the so-called Johnson Amendment, which was proposed by then-Senator Lyndon B. Johnson and passed in 1954. The purpose of the law was to stifle churches and other non-profits from campaigning and supporting politicians. Johnson in effect stifled political dissent in the church in accordance with his own political ambitions. Trump is ready to lift that gag order and unleash the political populism of the evangelical church.

Thus, it appears that the waning of multiculturalism and the rise of a nationalist populism indicates the dawn of a post-secular age. Despite the sporadic protests to the contrary, a Trump presidency signals to the wider culture that it is now open season on political correctness. And as far as I'm concerned, it couldn't have come soon enough.

CHAPTER 6

Trump, Education, and the Coming "War on Science"

Shortly after the election, Lawrence Krauss, professor at Arizona State University, opined in *The New Yorker* that the Trump administration is declaring a "war on science."[8] With the nomination of Betsy DeVos as education secretary, Krauss foregrounds education as part of this battle:

> DeVos is a fundamentalist Christian with a long history of opposition to science. If her faith shapes her policies—and there is evidence that it will—she could shape science education decisively for the worse, by systematically depriving young people, in an era where biotechnology will play a key economic and health role worldwide, of a proper understanding of the very basis of modern biology: evolution.

---

[8]http://www.newyorker.com/tech/elements/donald-trumps-war-on-science.

He goes on: "The purpose of education is not to validate ignorance but to overcome it. It should be easy, therefore, for Congress to make sure that DeVos isn't planning to drive our educational system off a scientific cliff."

Other than failing to provide a single example of DeVos' *actual* conflict with science, the irony here is that Krauss appears to be living in the past, rather oblivious to the cultural currents sweeping us into a post-secular society. In light of these changes, dogmatic appeals to science/religion dichotomies and the oft cited pejoratives (e.g. fundamentalists) that accompany such appeals appear increasingly a matter of question begging, recalcitrantly resistant to addressing a more complex understanding of the relationship between the twin spheres of science and religion. So much of this banter is rooted in rather outdated and largely discredited Enlightenment redefinitions of religion and knowledge that are not merely suffering the scourge of wider society, but also the critical eye of the academy. Post-secular scholars are fully sympathetic with the growing contemporary skepticism towards secular claims over reality and the professionalized partisanship, comprised of judges and journalists, pundits and professors that functions as its mediating priesthood.

Now that society is less inclined to cordon off religious viewpoints from public discussion, the challenge facing education today is to think anew how such viewpoints inform the programs and curricular offerings, as well as the mission, vision, and values of public classrooms. There is further concern that the kind of knowledge offered by secularized education, inspired by its (faith!) commitment to scientific rationalism, is incurably sterile, indifferent, and apathetic, devoid of the capacity to awaken the moral imagination so central to human development.

Schools are increasingly turning to traditions such as contemplative practices as part of their curriculum offerings. Examples of such include mindfulness meditation, which is a Zen Buddhist-inspired practice akin to prayer, as taught in MindUP programs in schools throughout the nation. Such mindfulness has been called by Emily Horn the "new American religion."[9]

But more to the point, populations are taking matters into their own hands with the passage of school choice initiatives, which have the potential to change dramatically the national landscape of what is considered public education. For example, in Louisiana's program, 86% of those who received vouchers used them to enroll in private and parochial schools. It would seem rather obvious that devout practitioners of the classical monotheistic faiths such as Christianity and Judaism can hardly consent to the reductionist privatization of their convictions. Vouchers free populations to educate according to their own (often traditional) values.

And school choice is proving to be an issue capable of amassing a remarkably diverse constituency of supporters. Who would ever have imagined the Republican Senator and former presidential candidate Ted Cruz sharing the stage in solidarity with the ultra-liberal Democrat Representative Sheila Jackson Lee? But this is happening across the political spectrum with school choice. And with Trump's proposal to

[9]http://www.huffingtonpost.com/candy-gunther-brown-phd/mindfulness-meditation-in_b_6276968.html.

redirect $20 billion in federal education spending to school choice initiatives, it does appear that the nation is moving away from the monolithic secular curriculum envisioned by Krauss.

What all of this means of course is that with her support for school choice and the charter school movement, DeVos, who of course was confirmed by the senate, is far more in touch with current social and educational trends than is Krauss. In many respects, then, his article is little more than a partisan exhortation seeking to rouse his fellow troops for battle, garnered to defend faithfully the beliefs of a secular age. But if current social and educational trends continue, his call to arms aside, it does appear that the war has already been decided.

CHAPTER 7

Nationalism and the Coming Pro-Life Spring

Recently the Polish parliament proposed legislation that would have banned abortion from the nation. Poland already has one of the most restrictive laws in Europe, allowing for abortion in only three cases: rape, the risk of the life of the mother, and serious malformations in the fetus. While the proposed bill didn't pass, the Polish government continues to push for a new law that would result in a near total ban.

What many have overlooked is the fact that this conservative pro-life sentiment among legislatures is accompanying a resurgent nationalism among Poles. The most recent rounds of elections put Polish nationalists in charge, those who emphasize Poland's sovereignty in light of European Union and Eurasian pressures. And of course, we're seeing similar nationalist processes here at home in the U.S. along with comparable pro-life sentiments. It is not a coincidence that the nationalist candidate Donald Trump was also the staunch pro-life advocate, bolstered by his thoroughly pro-life running mate, Mike Pence

There have been a number of studies that corroborate this connection between nationalism and pro-life political policies. For example, during Italy's nationalist turn in the mid-twentieth century, abortion was condemned as a crime; but as Italy became more globalized and liberalized, so did its abortion policies, particularly in the 1970s. We see this also in post-war Germany: in Communist Eastern Germany, the abortion laws were very permissive, while Western Germany maintained rather restrictive abortion laws as a hangover from its nationalist period. By the mid-1980s, the Soviet Union had one of the highest rates of abortion among developed countries, some estimates indicate 115 abortions for every 100 births. However, in their post-Soviet nationalist turn, with the rise of the Russian Orthodox Church, Russia has turned increasingly pro-life. Vladimir Putin has banned abortion ads, signed legislation banning abortion after 12 weeks of pregnancy, and the Russian Orthodox Church is calling for an all-out ban of abortions.

So what's the connection between nationalism and pro-life sentiments?

What seems to be going on in nationalist movements among traditionally Christian nations is a process known as re-traditionalization, a mass nationalist blowback against the de-traditionalizing dynamics of secular globalization. As noted above, in the face of globalized threats to local and national identity, populations reassert their local symbols, customs, traditions, and religions as mechanisms of resistance against these de-traditionalizing tendencies.

In historically Christian societies, abortion is considered anathema, rooted in the fact that the Christian faith blossoms from the birth of the Christ child, which is also celebrated in what is traditionally known as the Feast of the Annunciation of the angel Gabriel to Mary on March 25th, nine months before Christmas. Christ is celebrated at the very moment of conception and thus abortion is completely contrary to the very notion of the human person defined in Christian terms.

And what we're finding is that even if abortion is still largely legal in historically Christian nations in the West, many doctors simply refuse to perform abortions for conscience sake, even if there's no legislation barring it. For example, in Croatia, back in November 1991, the largest hospital in Zagreb prohibited its doctors from performing abortions – despite there being no law against abortion – for conscience sake; so, this conscience prohibition, particularly the Catholic conscience, often supplements the lack of legislation in these nationalist turns.

Here in the U.S., we are seeing renewed pro-life sentiments accompanying a revitalized nationalism. For the last several years, Gallup Polls have suggested that there is a rather pronounced trend towards the pro-life position nationally. Even the recent 2015 poll, which was the first in seven years favoring the pro-choice position, had 55% of the respondents wanting all or most abortions illegal. At the local level, the Christian Right has been very effective in passing abortion restrictions. For example, targeted regulations of abortion providers, or TRAP laws, have more than doubled since 2000, such that today, there are six states and counting that are down to a single abortion clinic.

And all of this has been going on in a sense under the radar during eight years of the most pro-abortion administration in American history. News reports are observing frequently the decline of abortion throughout the heartland of America. Most recently, the Alabama Supreme Court ruled that unborn children deserve legal protection, and Kentucky legislatures are considering a late term abortion ban, all in the shadow of President Trump's reinstating the so-called "Mexico City Policy" banning international abortion funding.

If past trends are any indicators, the recent nationalist tailwinds blowing through our nation will continue to swing in an increasingly pro-life direction.

CHAPTER 8

Feminist Futility: Why the Women's March Promises a More Conservative Future

On Saturday, January 21, 2017, more than a million people turned out nationwide to demonstrate against President Donald Trump and his nationalist agenda. The so-called "Women's March on Washington" featured a number of prominent feminist speakers, such as Planned Parenthood's current president, Cecile Richards, touting the rights of women and the so-called LGBT community. While it was only President Trump's second day in office, organizers of Saturday's marches are promising a number of additional actions throughout his first 100 days.

While the event was covered by a seemingly adoring media, a rather obvious consequence of feminist ideals has gone largely ignored, one that ironically promises a far more conservative future.

According to a recent demographic study by University of London Professor Eric Kaufmann, there is a significant demographic deficit between secularists and conservative religionists.[10] For example, in the U.S., while self-identified secular women averaged only 1.5 children per couple in 2002, conservative evangelical women averaged 2 to 3 children per couple, which amounts to a 28 percent fertility advantage. Now Kaufmann notices that this demographic deficit has dramatic effects over time. In a population evenly divided, these numbers indicate that conservative evangelicals would increase from 50 to 62.5 percent of the population in a single generation. In two generations, their number would increase to 73.5 percent, and over the course of 200 years, they would represent 99.4 percent.

Kaufmann noticed further that the more religiously conservative, the more children. For example, the Amish double in population every twenty years, and are projected to number over a million in the U.S. and Canada in just a few decades. We're seeing a similar trend among Mormons, who have averaged a 40 percent growth per decade, which means that by the end of the century, there will be as many as 300 million Mormons in the world, or six percent of the world's population. And note: Mormons vote overwhelmingly Republican.

Now in stark contrast to all of this, Kaufmann's data projects that secularists consistently exemplify a low fertility rate of around 1.5 percent per couple, which is significantly below the replacement level of 2.1 percent. And so he sees a steady decline of secular populations after 2030 or 2050 to potentially no more than a mere 14 to 15 percent of the

---

[10] Eric Kaufmann, *Shall the Religious Inherit the Earth? Demography and Politics in the Twenty-First Century* (London: Profile Books, 2010).

American population. He notices that similar projections apply to Europe as well.

So why is this happening? Why are secularists in effect disappearing off the face of the earth? Well, in an ironic twist, it's precisely because of what the Women's March was advocating: that a woman's freedom means relegating motherhood to a mere lifestyle choice and nothing more. These women refuse to be pigeonholed into some foreordained maternal vocation; motherhood is not a divine calling, it is a choice, one made by the woman herself and no one else.

Well, the demonstrators most certainly can have it their way, but not without dramatic demographic consequences to the civilizational significance of their movement. Kaufmann calls this demographic consequence "the soft underbelly of secularism." Here Kaufmann is channeling the early twentieth century sociologist Emile Durkheim, who analyzed societies in terms of their innate futility. Durkheim was fascinated with the question of why some societies and cultures succeed over time while others falter. For example, why did Christianity succeed and Baal worship fade into extinction? Durkheim inquired as to whether there was an inherent futility to the burgeoning secular society in Europe; is there something inherent in secularism that basically guarantees its demise?

Well, Kaufmann in effect says, 'yes', namely, demography. And this is because secular liberalism entails its own "demographic contradiction," the affirmation of the secular individual, one characterized by personal autonomy, *necessitates* the freedom not to reproduce. A secular person – male, female, and now the alphabet soup gender categories – is under no moral obligation to procreate. The link between sex and procreation having been broken, modernist reproduction translates into mere personal preference. It thus turns out that the radical individualism so celebrated and revered by our feminist demonstrators is in fact the agent by which their ideology implodes. This is the futility of feminism.

And so, while the litany of Saturday's speakers touted a national renewal of feminist ideals, in the end, the irony to the Women's March on Washington is that such a demonstration promises only a far more conservative future.

CONCLUSION

The basic argument that I presented in Part I of this book is that the Trump presidency is part of a larger worldwide nationalist, populist, and traditionalist blowback against the anticultural processes of globalization and its secular aristocracy. These nationalist, populist, and traditionalist trends are undermining the fundamental tenets of secularization and in effect forging the emergence of a post-secular world.

In Part II, we got a glimpse of what a post-secular world is beginning to look like. The Christian Right are more politically active than ever on a global scale; political correctness is giving way to a far more cooperative relationship between church and state united in a renewed civic nationalism; religion is being increasingly invited back into our public school system primarily through the school-choice movement; pro-life sentiments and policies are on the rise, and pro-family commitments have resulted in a decisive conservative Christian demographic edge over the waning secular population.

The old secular order, rooted in a rotted-out modernity, is collapsing. And in its place, is a new political order rooted in nation, culture, and tradition. The election of Donald J. Trump as President of the United States was merely one, albeit a highly significant, indicator of this tectonic shift, a shift that is even now reshaping the global map into a post-secular world.

A new conservative nationalist age has begun.

Thank you again for purchasing this book!

I hope this book helped to awaken you to what the 2016 election was ultimately about: the dawning of a new post-secular age.

If you enjoyed this book, then I'd like to ask you for a favor: Would you be kind enough to leave a review for this book on Amazon? I would so greatly appreciate it!

Thank you so much, and may God richly bless you!

Steve Turley

www.turleytalks.com

Check Out My Other Books

Below you'll find some of my other popular books that are popular on Amazon. Simply go to the links below to check them out. Alternatively, you can visit my author page on Amazon to see my other works.

- *Movies and the Moral Imagination: Finding Paradise in Films* http://amzn.to/2zjghJj
- *Classical vs. Modern Education: A Vision from C.S. Lewis* http://amzn.to/2opDZju
- *Health Care Sharing Ministries: How Christians are Revolutionizing Medical Cost and Care* http://amzn.to/2B2Q8B2
- *Ever After: How to Overcome Cynical Students with the Role of Wonder in Education* http://amzn.to/2jbJI78
- *The Face of Infinite of Love: Athanasius on the Incarnation* http://amzn.to/2oxULNM
- *Stressed Out: Learn How an Ancient Christian Practice Can Relieve Stress and Overcome Anxiety* http://amzn.to/2kFzcpc
- *Wise Choice: Six Steps to Godly Decision Making* http://amzn.to/2CMu1vH
- *Awakening Wonder: A Classical Guide to Truth, Goodness, and Beauty* http://amzn.to/2ziKR5H
- *Worldview Guide for* A Christmas Carol http://amzn.to/2BCcKHO
- *The Ritualized Revelation of the Messianic Age: Washings and Meals in Galatians and 1 Corinthians* http://amzn.to/2B0mGvf

If the links do not work, for whatever reason, you can simply search for these titles on the Amazon website to find them.

About www.TurleyTalks.com

Are we seeing the revitalization of Christian civilization?

For decades, the world has been dominated by a process known as globalization, an economic and political system that hollows out and erodes a culture's traditions, customs, and religions, all the while conditioning populations to rely on the expertise of a tiny class of technocrats for every aspect of their social and economic lives.

Until now.

All over the world, there's been a massive blowback against the anti-cultural processes of globalization and its secular aristocracy. From Russia to Europe and now in the U.S., citizens are rising up and reasserting their religion, culture, and nation as mechanisms of resistance against the dehumanizing tendencies of secularism and globalism.

And it's just the beginning.

The secular world is at its brink, and a new traditionalist age is rising.

Join me each week as we examine these worldwide trends, discover answers to today's toughest challenges, and together learn to live in the present in light of even better things to come.

So hop on over to www.TurleyTalks.com and have a look around. Make sure to sign-up for our weekly Email Newsletter where you'll get lots of free giveaways, private Q&As, and tons of great content. Check out our YouTube channel (www.youtube.com/c/DrSteveTurley) where you'll understand current events in light of conservative trends to help you flourish in your personal and professional life. And of course, 'Like' us on Facebook and follow us on Twitter.

Thank you so much for your support and for your part in this cultural renewal.

About the Author

Steve Turley (PhD, Durham University) is an internationally recognized scholar, speaker, and classical guitarist. He is the author of *Awakening Wonder: A Classical Guide to Truth, Goodness, and Beauty* (Classical Academic Press) and *The Ritualized Revelation of the Messianic Age: Washings and Meals in Galatians and 1 Corinthians* (T&T Clark). Steve blogs on the church, society and culture, education, and the arts at TurleyTalks.com. He is a faculty member at Tall Oaks Classical School in Bear, DE, where he teaches Theology, Greek, and Rhetoric, and Professor of Fine Arts at Eastern University. Steve lectures at universities, conferences, and churches throughout the U.S. and abroad. His research and writings have appeared in such journals as *Christianity and Literature, Calvin Theological Journal, First Things, Touchstone*, and *The Chesterton Review*. He and his wife, Akiko, have four children and live in Newark, DE, where they together enjoy fishing, gardening, and watching *Duck Dynasty* marathons.

Made in the USA
Columbia, SC
18 August 2020

16723844R00039